A Shepherd Boy Who Trusted God

A True Story from the Bible
B. W. Reads

Arete Publishing, LLC

To my children and grandchildren.

A Shepherd Boy Who Trusted God
Copyright © 2024 by B. W. Reads

Published by Arete Publishing, LLC
www.AretePublishing.com
All rights reserved.

ISBN 978-1-964118-02-4 Hardcover Premium
ISBN 978-1-964118-07-9 Hardcover
ISBN 978-1-964118-04-8 Paperback

Scripture quotations are taken from the *Holy Bible*, New Living Translation, Copyright © 1996, 2004, 2015 by Tyndale House Foundation. Used by permission of Tyndale House Publishers, Carol Stream, Illinois 60188. All rights reserved.

No part of this book may be reproduced in any form, or by any means electronic or mechanical, including photocopying, recording, or by any information storage or retrieval system, without written permission of the copyright holder B. W. Reads and Arete Publishing, LLC, except in the case of brief quotations in articles and reviews, or as provided by USA copyright law.

Hello! I'm Birdy the Wordy.

Today we're going to read the true story about David and Goliath. It's an exciting adventure filled with lots of action and a surprise ending.

Let's see what happened on that fateful day.

The vast armies of Israel and the Philistines gathered for battle in the Valley of Elah.

Facing each other on opposite hills, they stood firmly, their banners fluttering in the breeze.

As the tension mounted, a massive figure emerged from the ranks of the Philistines: a champion named Goliath, who towered over the other soldiers.

His armor shone in the sunlight, and he carried a heavy spear, confident in his strength and prowess.

Goliath issued a challenge to the Israelite army, calling for a single combatant to face him in battle. His strong, deep voice boomed slowly across the valley:

"I defy the armies of Israel today! Send me a man who will fight me!"

But nobody in the camp was brave enough to face the giant.

Day after day, Goliath taunted the Israelite army and their leader, King Saul, daring them to send someone to fight him.

The Israelites were terrified and dismayed, and their morale plummeted.

Then a young shepherd boy named David arrived at the camp, bringing supplies to his brothers who were fighting in the army.

He quickly went to see his kin, and while he was greeting them, he heard Goliath taunting the Israelite soldiers.

David, hearing Goliath's defiant words, was outraged. He then asked the soldiers who were standing nearby:

"What will a man get for killing this Philistine and ending his defiance of Israel? Who is this pagan Philistine anyway, that he is allowed to defy the armies of the living God?"

Despite his youth and inexperience, David, the lowly shepherd boy, was filled with faith in God's power to protect him.

So he informed King Saul that he would fight the giant.

"Don't worry about this Philistine," David told Saul. "I'll go fight him!"

King Saul, initially hesitant, eventually allowed David to face Goliath, trusting in God's protection of the lad.

A SHEPHERD BOY WHO TRUSTED GOD 11

Armed with a sling and five smooth stones, David approached the giant with unwavering confidence.

Goliath was indignant that a small shepherd boy would challenge him. He sneered with contempt.

"Am I a dog," he roared at David, "that you come at me with a stick? . . . Come over here, and I'll give your flesh to the birds and wild animals!"

David, remaining undeterred and confident, boldly shouted back to the giant warrior:

"You come to me with sword, spear, and javelin, but I come to you in the name of the LORD of Heaven's Armies — the God of the armies of Israel, whom you have defied. . . . This is the LORD's battle, and he will give you to us!"

As Goliath charged, David skillfully hurled a stone from his sling, striking the giant in the forehead.

The soldiers watching from both sides of the valley were shocked at what happened next.

Goliath, stunned and weakened, fell to the ground.

David then seized the opportunity to finish the job with Goliath's own sword. It was truly a remarkable feat!

The Israelite army, emboldened by David's victory against the giant, charged the Philistine forces and defeated them decisively.

The story of David and Goliath became a symbol of faith, courage, and the power of the Lord to overcome even the most formidable obstacles. And it was accomplished through the bravery of a small shepherd boy who placed all his trust in God.

And that, my friends, is what happened. You can read all about the true story of David and Goliath in the Bible.

Turn to 1 Samuel 17, and prepare yourself for a wonderful adventure. Goodbye and may God richly bless you!